For Dorsey Blue.
—B. M.

In memory of my father.
—S. L.

Henry Holt and Company, *Publishers since 1866*

Henry Holt® is a registered trademark of Macmillan Publishing Group, LLC

120 Broadway, New York, NY 10271 • mackids.com

This text is adapted from *Falter* by Bill McKibben,
originally published in 2019 by Henry Holt and Company.

Our books may be purchased in bulk for promotional, educational, or business use. Please
contact your local bookseller or the Macmillan Corporate and Premium Sales Department
at (800) 221-7945 ext. 5442 or by email at MacmillanSpecialMarkets@macmillan.com.

Library of Congress Cataloging-in-Publication Data is available.

First edition, 2022

The artwork was rendered digitally.

Printed in China by Hung Hing Off-set Printing Co. Ltd., Heshan City, Guangdong Province

ISBN 978-1-250-75515-5

1 3 5 7 9 10 8 6 4 2

WE ARE BETTER TOGETHER

BILL McKIBBEN

ILLUSTRATIONS BY
STEVIE LEWIS

GODWINBOOKS

HENRY HOLT AND COMPANY

NEW YORK

The human game is a
team sport.

It took a band, a clan, a community,
to raise humans to adulthood.

We hunted together in groups.

With our complex language,
we're able to keep track of one another.

When we work together, we can do incredible things.

We can harness the power of the sun.

We can reforest the land.

We can help lost sea turtles find
their way to the ocean.

We can explore the farthest reaches of space. And looking back, we can see how we are changing our planet.

It is a beautiful, fragile place—
worthy of protection.

We can accept with grace that each
of us has a moment and a place.

That our humanness is important.

We have the tools to allow us to stand up to the powerful and the reckless.

REDUCE
REUSE

T'S OUR WORLD

THIS I
CLIM
REVOLU

ONE
EARTH

OCEANS
ARE
RISING

THERE IS
NO
PLANET B

TECT
OLAR
EARS

We know the value of love.

It's love that works to feed the hungry.

FREE
MEALS
TODAY

It's love that comes together in defense of sea turtles
and sea ice and all else around us that is good.

It's love that lets each of us see we're not the most important thing on Earth, and makes us okay with that.

It's love that
welcomes us imperfect
into the world.

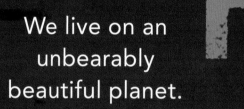

We live on an
unbearably
beautiful planet.

A planet that needs us
humans to play together,
to cooperate.

RIDE
FOR

CLIMATE RID

ZERO EMISSIONS

CYCLE 4 OUR KIDS

SMALL FARMS

We're capable of acting together to do remarkable things.

So we'd best get started soon.

FROM THE AUTHOR

This book is a celebration of the power of human cooperation. When we work together, we can do incredible things. We are radically remaking our planet, and fast. In the thirty years I've been working on the climate change crisis, we've seen all twenty of the hottest years ever recorded. It is critical that we act collectively to protect our beautiful, fragile world. I have confidence that we can.

Some of that conviction stems from human ingenuity—watching the rapid spread of a technology as world-changing as the solar panel cheers me daily. And much of that conviction rests on events in my own life over the past few decades. I've immersed myself in movements working for change, and I helped found a group, 350.org, that grew into the first planetwide climate campaign. Though we haven't beaten the fossil fuel industry, we've organized demonstrations in every country on the globe save North Korea, and with our many colleagues around the world, we've won some battles. I've been to a thousand rallies, and along the way, I've come to believe that we have the tools to stand up to the powerful.

Many people in many places have played many roles in the movement—especially, tellingly, those in the poorest places hardest hit by environmental change. It's a movement increasingly led by kids, Indigenous nations, communities of color. It has been a great privilege to see up close that, even against the biggest and richest forces on the planet, this technology of nonviolence can prove its power.

We really do live on an unbearably beautiful planet. Even with seven billion of us, the planet remains an astonishing collection not just of cities and suburbs, but of mountains and ice and forests and ocean. I've been to the highest year-round human habitation, the Rongbuk Monastery in Tibet, and stared up from its rocky ground at Everest overhead, its summit so high that it sticks into the jet stream and unrolls a long pennant of white cloud. I've wandered the Antarctic Peninsula, watching glaciers calve icebergs with a thunderous roar. I've climbed on the endless lava fields of Iceland and watched the magma pour into the Pacific Ocean from Kilauea, in Hawaii, birthing new land before my eyes. I've seen the steam puffing from the top of Mount Rainier and wondered if I'd managed to climb it the day it would erupt. And I've lain on my stomach in my backyard, watching beetles wander by, watching dew hang on stalks of grass. I've seen penguins, I've watched whales, I've played with my dog.

We live on a planet, and it's infinitely glorious.

Let's figure out how to solve the problems we face. Let's be, for a while, true optimists. Let's act together to do remarkable things.

Bill McKibben

FROM THE ILLUSTRATOR

During our short time on this planet, we are often too busy, stressed, or distracted to appreciate the present moment. The sound of the birds chirping as the sun rises, the river flowing, and the leaves swaying in the wind are subtle gifts the earth shares with us each day. Becoming aware of important issues like climate change comes from observing our present moment.

I was late to "doing my part" to help the planet. For me, it happened when I left my job in the big city to pursue a life on the road. I sold everything I owned, moved into a van, and strived to live simply, to contribute less waste, own fewer things, support organic and healthy soil practices, and be a better steward for the land and the planet. When you spend all your time outdoors, you become more conscious of the earth and the effects of climate change. Some moments during my travels affected me deeply. In Oregon, I remember walking through a dry forest that had been completely devastated by fire. In 2017, I spent a summer in a campground in Juneau, Alaska. While my partner maintained trails in the backcountry, I would hike to nearby glaciers. Each time, I was shocked to see how much the glaciers had receded. Driving through farmland in the Midwest, I witnessed planes spraying harmful pesticides on hundreds of acres of crops, completely disregarding the health of the soil and essentially destroying all life but the plant itself. It made me feel so sad. So I strived to do better.

However, I realize that to care for the earth comes from a place of privilege. Part of the dilemma of climate change is directly related to poverty and harsh living conditions on this planet. So many humans are not in the right mindset to prioritize the environment over their own basic needs. Educating others in a constructive and helpful way is our best way forward.

I know what you're thinking: *How can I significantly enact change? I'm just one person.* But that's how it all begins. Once you change your mindset and lead by example, others will feel inspired to follow. It can be as simple as bringing a reusable bag to the grocery store or supporting brands that align with your ethics. Stay diligent and positive. Share your stories. And remember to enjoy the present moment. We can do this together.

Stevie Lewis